The Three Hedgehogs

by Ned Pike and Freya Pike

illustrated by Luke Jurevicius

Harcourt Achieve

Rigby • Saxon • Steck-Vaughn

www.HarcourtAchieve.com
1.800.531.5015

Characters

Ruttel

Zed

DD

Contents

Chapter 1

Garbage Hill

On the top of a hill in an old camper lived three fat hedgehogs. All three hedgehogs were fat, but one was much fatter than the others. His name was Ruttel.

The camper sat on a hill, but it was not
a grassy hill.

It was a hill of garbage — a great
big hill of stinking trash. It was
almost a mountain. Every day the hill
grew bigger.

At the bottom of the hill was a harbor.
Every day at 4 o'clock a boat arrived.

It was loaded with garbage from the city. The captain raised the flinging machine up. He turned it on.

The garbage was hurled into the air. It flew up to the top of the hill.

Most of it would fly in through the window of the camper. Fff - fff - ttt!

That is why Ruttel was so fat. He sat in the camper with his big mouth wide open. The garbage poured through the window and landed in his wide-open mouth.

Some of the garbage bounced off the walls. That's what Zed and DD, the other two hedgehogs, ate.

One day part of the hill slid away from under the camper. The camper began to lean. It began to wobble.

Chapter 2

Time to Run

The three hedgehogs sat very still.

Ruttel whispered, "I think we'd better jump out."

Zed and DD agreed.

"On the count of three, run for the door. One . . . two . . . three . . . " said Ruttel.

But Zed and DD ran on the count of
two. They reached the door and tried
to leap out. They got stuck! Their
bottoms wiggled in the doorway.

The camper began to fall. It crashed
down, and the two hedgehogs popped
out. They landed headfirst in two old
pickle jars.

The camper slid down the slushy slope.
It bounced and crunched its way
through years of garbage.

A large car-crushing machine hung low over the garbage. The camper headed straight for it.

Its jagged teeth tore through the camper like a can-opener. The roof totally ripped off.

Ruttel clung to his beanbag chair. He thought, "I'm done for, now."

He looked up at the clear blue sky. "What a lovely day it is today," he said.

Chapter 3

First Flight

Faster and faster the camper roared down the hill. It felt as if it would break into a million pieces. Ruttel's bones rattled, and his teeth shook.

Near the bottom of the hill, the camper hit a wooden ramp. It slid down the smooth wood and up the other side. The camper flew up into the sky and out across the sea.

Ruttel looked out the window at the
seagulls. He thought, "What lovely
birds they are to fly with me."

24

The seagulls squawked and ducked out
of his way.

The camper landed — *splash* — into the water. Ruttel shot up into the air. As he exploded out of the camper, he began to flap his tiny arms.

In the middle of the sky, he thought,
"I like it up here. I must come up here
again one day."

Then he began to fall. Ruttel looked
down. The camper came closer and
closer.

Puff-fff-ftt went the beanbags as he
landed in them. They burst into a cloud
of tiny, white balls.

Ruttel rolled over onto his back.

"I must learn to fly. This really has been a beautiful day."

Glossary

beanbags
large cushions used as chairs

camper
a trailer you can live in

car-crushing machine

a machine that squeezes cars until they are flat

harbor

deep water close to shore where boats can tie up

hedgehogs

small mammals that have sharp spines on their back

jagged
sharp, spiky edge
that can cut

pickle
a vegetable kept
in vinegar

ramp
a sloping surface
that joins two levels

slushy
muddy, greasy

squawked
made a loud, harsh
noise

Ned Pike and Freya Pike

Ned, 11, and Freya, 10, came up with this story on a long car journey down the coast. It's a good way to pass the time. The story turns out best when you keep asking the question — "What else could happen?"

Luke Jurevicius